Rough Passage

Rough Passage

Poems by

Michael Brokensha

To order additional copies of this book, contact:
Xlibris Corporation
1-888-795-4274
www.Xlibris.com
Orders@Xlibris.com
49359

CONTENTS

For Zara, Zoso and Marcela Tavarez Cuevas.

Acknowledgements

Thanks are due to Les Parsons and Jackie Ashley-Lahiff for their comments and encouragement and to Alison Nash and Patricia Clarke for their valuable help. My thanks also go to Christiwild for allowing me to use the cover photo. Further acknowledgements are found in the Appendix.

'My doubts stand in a circle around every word.'
Franz Kafka-Diaries of Franz Kafka.

Rough Passage

What tutors are there for a young child
When parents are absent for whatever reason?

Baby lambs, separated from or untaken to their
Mothers, receive the hours long devotion
Of the farmer raising them as pets
Before they are let loose on the flock.

Would that a child have loving grandparents
To make up for such umbilical loss,
Or that ubiquitous auntie
To shield it from embryonic sensitivity.

Yet I suspect the sever often sears deep
Even with heartfelt refuge.

Sometimes he used to lie awake an albino mute,
huddled up and hiding from moonlight,
alarmed by the midnight foxes death dance shriek.

Or so it seemed.

And then he imagined blood
and once dreamt of a vase
of red roses on the black enamelled top
of a grand piano and woke up
in his dream with a start, clutching
a skin in his sweaty palms.

A Thames lighterman once showed me
His foetal cloak and told me such a skin
Was a mother's good luck gift
To her young sailor boy off to sea.

That said, how different things
Could easily have been, to be
Offered such protection from this passage
Without such troubled dreams.

Of a night like this.

The street lamp bares its nippled light
On the silhouetted couple at the bus stop.
Damp the cold sweat glazed tarmac
And the grass moist with the livered
Bile of remnant autumn.
Brown leaves slug-like in their decay
Nestle in a swathe of moonlight
Cold blue in its affection.

A passing car, incandescent in
The loitering light fog of evening,
Condenses the air with puffs of phantom vapours.
The couple barely speak in their frozen art form embrace
For they are faceless,
A monument and memory for any time,
For any place.

The night is silent in waiting for silhouettes,
Silhouette of a bus, its warm deck of hope
And home for young lovers, Silhouette
Of a jewelled evening
In a squirreled nest of a cinema seat,
Silhouette of forgotten values and neo-50's romantic perfume
Of a night like this. Silhouette of a time before these dark skies.

The slow primal pulse of this vespered world,
Adagio in requiem,
Pristine in its majesty and calm measure,
Awakens the imagination
And sharpens the senses.
Now the moon is gothic high and eerie bright
Above the swirling night-time mist and bliss of the lovers
Final embrace.

The sweet kiss of promises on the shifting air
That can so easily fade in the first blades of sunlight.
The loosening grip before the parting, a necromantic
Void filled with new born feelings
And silhouettes of ghosts,
Tremulous yet tender,
Of a night like this.

Sighs and Whispers

The house holds its secrets.
Search long and hard and you will
Find little prows of silver,
Magnetic monuments
Of unspoken memories,
The delicate dance of dust
To the song of ancient hearts,
Unfolded and wrapped around the tongues
Of men and women in spoken moments
Of meant to be truth.

The house will utter a slight
Cough at its core,
A feint auraic tremor.

In this house my parents
May have dusted off the skin of their liaison,
In unguarded moments,
Or stamped their passion
On the crust of walls
And floorboards.

What passed between their lips
Lay to rest on Edwardian mantle pieces
And broken mantle clocks.
My grandfather's hands clipping hair
And exchanging bookies bets
In the canopies of cupboards
And under stairs lairs.
My grandmother's wistful
Sighs and heavy legs as age bolted
Her spirit to the big brass bed,
Her mattress damp with deeds.
The dark heavy wardrobes and
Tallboy mirrors,
All mothballed, a methyl sting,
A distant whisper.

Now there's a faint ray of light
Through the period stained glass
door.
The skylight is bright and bold
With youthful atoms bouncing
And swirling like a sprat sack of
Joy yet to settle in
The musty corners of the dead.
The prows of silver are still,
Still until a new generation
Furrows its way through sacred ground
Scattering silver dust on the salient
Draught to fall wherever.

Tattoo

The needlepoint a jagged burr,
The inscription blurred.
Blood memory blending with
Fading horizons.
What's on the inside comes out.
Emotion, a cyst of sweat,
A nerve blip on the brain,
Sculptured graft of skin.

He woke to a haunting Gaelic chant,
Ephemeral mystic whispers
Of cascading beauty across
The wide expanse, barren and mountainous,
That channelled down to the sea.
The wind and spray mixed with the mist
And sodden turf.
Perspiration was at his fingertips
Cooling the fire in the molten granite heart.
Metamorphic shale, a latent seam of
Feeling eroded to the surface elements.

The tattoo was bruised and numb.
The haunting whispers a tinnitus grief,
Ever so slight yet profound.
His body turning inside out.
His skin a gently weeping.

Love was a blurred tattoo on his arm that still bore her name.

SE14 /SE3

'Nothing like something happens anywhere.' Phillip Larkin—I Remember I Remember

Was that a friend I saw you
with at the bus stop?
The cold gripping tight,
squeezing heat from the soul,
waiting for the no.21 at New Cross Gate.
Silhouettes of passengers
and bright amber lights,
red buses corralling into one another,
the darkening dusk of late afternoon
English time, the traffic crawling over
Blackheath.

A fragile narrative. Lapidary of memory.
Ephemeral glimpses of a crestfallen
student walking a broken path
to a park bench near Deptford Creek,
later a smiling graduate.

Towering clouds of smoke and vapour.
Dancing at the Swan with a girl from Greece
or shuffling along Albany Street
to see a wizard of a Turkish car mechanic.

Ghost images.
The faint sound of horses from the old brewery,
the breath of alcohol and meths,
chips scattered and mushed outside the refuge,
sickly smells curdled on the cold wind,
the pixilated eyes of a drunk.
Who of us is free from our poison?
We queue up for it.

Joy and unimaginable expectation.
Scrimmaging in Deptford market,
arm held round a beautiful Jewish girlfriend.
Drinking jasmine tea with friends,
sitting on kaftan coats and a junket
of colourful scarves, playing jazz
in a basement band in Lewisham Way,
true life sketches
of a pavement artist before Joseph
was sold into slavery. Was her coat that beautiful?

Valency of loose association.
Young lovers on a
passing train from Waterloo.

*All is a constant loop, atmosphere of place
And self-made masquerades.*

Catch your bus friend,
be on your way.
And you? I see your
work is afoot and real,-
a measure of your defeat,
solace of walking the cold
streets of Deptford and ducking
into the warmth of the New Cross House.
A beautiful stripper dances to the faint
beat of a world in repetition
as old as you are in its worn out spinning.
And does it bring you some kind of cheer being
in out of the cold with words that
have the faint fragrance of survival?
Nothing is so like something.

Where rats scatter

"He not busy being born is busy dying."—Bob Dylan

The frosted cross and gravestones
In this churchyard mind.
The gravel path of crunched up stones,
The lych-gate where bier and coffin lay
In solitary state,
Cloistered from the light.
A nether world
Where the winter cold enters,
A sharp wind freezing the
Nerve blood gable nose.

A death state of after sense
Lying there,
Poll bearers at the four gates
To the wayward paths beyond,
Corporeal riches and meaningless noise.
The rats scatter, their beaded vision
Blinkered in this shadow world.
The atmosphere is remorseless,
The cold earth, the tendered heavens
Of snow clouds and dust.

At the edge of these horizons
A church door closes
As a congregation of collectors
Gather without compassion.

The coffin corpse is soon emptied of memories.
Drained away in the blood-blanched
State of constant grief and regrets.
Life's eternal rigor mortis.

Catering for the bad taste cooks

Do you remember the cream-sauce days
Of sole-modernity and lobster?
There at the Café Perigordine,
Where the butter-soaked, port-wrapped,
Puff-baked, ash-slaked truffles
Were washed away in a flood
Of Chateau Latour.
Half the world was starving then
When you picked mussels off the rocks
And gathered dandelions for the salad
Of health.
Oh! The innocent days before the slaughter.
Now strawberries whip cream
Off those stew-faced clichés.
Meat is beaten, frozen, weakened,
Garlic-killed, wine-braised, re-heated
And the germ-kill technique repeated,
In the medieval gut of our youth.
Chicken and bacon smelling of fish
Come starving and squealing
From the Academy of Butchers,
Who masquerade with Maxim hatchets
And Edwardian bloodstained aprons.
This is the new Aquitaine,
Here in the bouillabaisse dungeons
Of Charlotte Street and St Michel.
Now half the world is starving
For the other!

Extinction

From the shadows of my heart
What happens here turns to dust
In the atmosphere.

Through the glacial flow
Blue and green
Rushing waters of melting ice in chasms
Unseen.

Through the giants trees
Scaling high into the sky
Swirling condensation
Vaporising and drying
Dying from the top down.

The spider dances like a clown
Writhes and shrivels
To a brittle snap,
Just like the coral
Blanched and bleached
In the too warm seas
Of the swelling breeze.

Think what is happening here,
Think what is happening to you and me?

In my soul god knows
I am crying for the children of the night
I am sighing for the hopeless dream.
In my mind I forge trinkets of rusted trust
Hold out a hand as if blind
And topple forward to that precipice.

All the while I hear the Angels.
A weeping or a laughing?

Harold's gone

On a nearby hillside
four horses were silhouetted against the evening sky.
A few drops of rain fell like the drips of conscience from a previous time.

But now there are no sacred values and nothing to look back on.

On a fascia gargoyle of the village church
a crow perched,
his beak clogged with black coal dust.

With almost human askance the bird registered the distaste
and indigestibility of the gluepy carbon sediment,
and jerked instinctively, convulsively for fear of choking.

It was the twilight of Remembrance Day.
A small gathering drifted from the churchyard
to the gothic wrought iron gate.

Impaled on the gate
was a cross of the crucifixion.
Cold comfort to the dwindling congregation.

The crow put to flight at the sound of the iron gate creaking.
Bits of coal dust dropped to the ground as it managed several caws
of irritation.

That day Harold had been buried.
Dear Harold, sweet Harold,
Harold who in the long months of his death throe
would constantly mutter, "Oh dear, Oh dear, Oh dear."
Uttered between short gasps of breath.
"Never mind, can't complain, far more worse off than me,"
he would oft refrain, instinctively, convulsively,
in plaintive apologia and blessed meek submission.

"Complain you bastard! you poor dear bastard!
Why not?—your body and mind so riddled
with cancerous affliction. You have every right to rant and rave
as you have ever done,
To bear witness to the hideous nature of your torturous demise.
Why?—then witness the bloody minded in this world
as they caw to kingdom come. Best die in the heat of battle with your soul
on fire
and not in blessed meek submission for what you shall inherit."

But who am I to talk? Who am I to know
what pain you were going through? Your death so imminent,
so long imminent. I just administered kind
faith and a loving hand before your heart surrendered
quietly to its armchair death.

Were you immaculately dressed then in best tweed suit,
polished shoes and tie, a gentleman for all occasions?
I believe so for your manners were made in heaven
and the world is lost without your kind.

Now deep shadows crowd in, in gormenghast madness.
As for the rest of us, how long have we surrendered before we die?
Sometimes it feels like I have been all my life ill and trying to get better.
Faint hope against hope. Trying is no salvation.
Still never mind. Far more worse of than my kind!

As the iron gate shut and the congregation
dispersed, the crow baulked in flight and landed quickly
to keel over mortally afflicted.
The four horses on the hillside stirred at the crow's descent.
One horse kicked its hooves and flicked up its tail erect before cantering away
some distance. The others followed.

Nightime was gathering.

Rusting from inside

Have you ever sat in a meeting
Full of purpose and meaning only for your
Bladder to prolapse and leak?

No?

Then maybe someday, for even
If the fabric of your world
Is built of steel,
Rust is eating at your kidney will.
Mammoth tankers corroding in salty oceans
Will break up on the jagged crumbling shores of your heart.
Sky buses flying at monstrous effluent speeds
Will rattle and crash in the congested bronchioles
Of your languid lungs.
Lost and out of puff, the earth that is your soul will collapse
And the heavens will fall.

Was it a shock to the system
To know that we and particularly women
will discriminate
As well as castigate and abdicate
Before your princely majesty
And dethrone you at the whim of true
Selection.
The shadow vortexes of the lower chakras
Integrated with the mindful renaissance of the higher levels
Hint at some salvation
Beyond the bravado and innocence
Of youthful looks and naïve smiles.

But who will hold your hand when you are old
And shuffling incontinent.
Who do you want to care?
Not some young intern or sassy nurse
Full of god knows know-how,
Brutal in their caring bedside banter,
Indifferent and arrogant with the vanity
Of their age and immortality.
For you are condemned and consigned
Near as you are to your sell-by date,
No matter what rectitude of mind will exhilarate
The tongue and twist the crooked beak of meaning
In your favour.

Are you grumpy like those heroes on TV
And really not that clever?

Then let me dress you up
Yves St Laurent looks and style.
Intelligent glasses, jet-black hair
And olive skin. Eyes like carbon nuggets,
Black holes to a fathomless mind,
Wearing jeans and jackets and shirts
In loose rangy rhythm.
A containment riveted
To your undoubted talent
With enough hair to satisfy any changing style.
Yet assured enough to hold thoracic truth
In indefinable insouciance.—a stillness inside
That could cross a raging river but the wisdom not to.

Imagine again when you were young and thin
With juicy shiny lips and the fragrant smell
of a healthy spleen and stomach.
All manner of guises shaped your grace and inner favour
Where cultured hands bronzed nicely
In the sun and love and fear
Where framed in optimistic fervour,
Young energy and vibrant jing
Shooting seed over the pillow case
Whilst in your lover's
Rampant joyful embrace.

But the stains are now cold and congealed aren't they?
And no grace and favour on my part can raise the dead
From nostalgic coffins.

So you sit there as they discuss you with meaning,
Looking for some comfortable route
Whilst you bleed inside
And the world burns again somewhere in the
Middle East.
Puny pontificating,
Trying to disguise the fact that you and they are
Rusting from inside.
All is spoken with the smile of a creased up lie.

In that moment you could so easily become that
Terrorist you so despise.
Couldn't you?

Adios 1

Present Simple/Present Continuous.—TEFL Drill.

She is a girl
He is a boy
She is walking
He is thinking
She is beautiful
He is fair
She is looking
He is dreaming
She is contemptuous
He is embarrassed
She has a car
He has a book
She drives away
He turns a page.

Adios 2

*"your eyes are deeper than time
say a love that won't rhyme without words." Small Faces—Tin Soldier*

Stone Free

They caught him those eyes, that look.
A hook of recognition,
Canopic senses of pre-conception
Distilled from fathomless urns.
The gestation of embryonic resonance.

He had no choice for he was drawn
With only the will to look away,
A will that grows stronger with the tepid beat of his heart,
The slight glow of a dying ember.
What memories are evoked if any by that look?
But a tired listless ache when once excited.

He can describe them
Those eyes, the dewy blue whites
Catching the light in shadows grace,
Brown unblemished orbs,
Doe like yet searching,
Asking questions of him
In undisturbed gaze.

They touch him beyond words,

For they are now dumb, he and she.
Their alien tongues
No echo of a chord, no musical muse to resonate
A grace, a smile.
They are inadequate, only knowing
The attraction
Not the resolution
Just the gaze;
A mirror reflection
On the tapestry of light,
A refraction of being that aches to be touched.

In the past he would dance the dance to thread a connection
Beyond this soundless sightless seam.
Now he looks in a seconds wonder
And brushes the fragile dust from his eyes,
Wipes the mirror clean yet be it smeared.

Her look, her longing, her questions
Will be answered by her god,
In breath, in love, in life, in hope.
He awaits no meeting in that other land
Where bridled tongues
Are loosed reigned in mellifluous tones.
He can only speak on present terms
Even if those eyes were once his destiny
To overwhelm him.
Now he turns away with only a faint yearning,
Stone free but crippled,
A sarcophagus of brittle spirits lay behind him.

Adios 3

"You are a look in your eye, a dream passing by in the sky." Small Faces—Tin Soldier

The sound of wild regret

She whispers her wishes through the language of her eyes,
Sultry yet coy, almost a blemish on an unblemished beauty.
She is the bounty of his youthful dreams,
The promise he made himself.
She stands there on some distant horizon, touching the sky
As near as the night to his waking dreams.
The sheen on her lips, the smooth mocha tone of her tanned skin,
Her blouse parts, her cleavage pouts milky smooth perfect breasts,
Her long legs languish their shapely promise.
The clouds part and their eyes catch each other for a brief moment in affinity.

The intelligence of attraction,
Seeing, unseeing. Knowing, unknowing.
The moment of anticipation, of action or non-action.
In any time or place they could have spoken, they could have kissed,
They could have waltzed their lives together
In bliss or remiss.
Chance is such a simple twist.

But for now, what is the sound of wild regret?
The sound of bridled desire?
A wiry pulse taught and tightening around the heart?
Where is the love?
Deep inside?
The solitude, the torture of strength?
What is the sound of wild regret as their eyes part?
Never to meet again as the clouds obscure the view.

The black, black rain. the silver light,
Mountains of fire and a desert of dust,
Funnels of fury,—this is the sound of wild regret,
Molten stone frozen,
Monastic romance. The bush clover
Grips the red sand.
The wind rustles the fetid heat to flame.
Cool white buildings, the clean space, the dance of freedom
On this florid moment,
A lost opportunity,
A lifetime over,
Adios.

Fusion and fission

A buzzard floats high
On the breeze over Kit Hill.
Far off the snow white tors of Dartmoor
Rest against a billow of background clouds.
The midday sun is warm and sharp.

Distant cars, mute and serene
Wind over rolling roads.

The bracken shakes in the chilly
Gusts of wind though tall
Barren tress stand stark and still
Above the cropped hedgerows.

A patchwork of green and yellow and brown fields
Stretch in undulating majesty
For miles, patiently waiting
The first twitch of Spring.

Two robins alert and flirty
All fluff tails and flighty
Flit past.

Shadows of clouds comb across
The landscape.

In distorted perspective,
The distant sea seems to tower above
The coast and cranes of Devonport.

The Tamar silent, silver and sultry
In the sun yet cold grey in cloud,
Snakes through
The valley.

Ice and fire
Mingle across this land,
Waiting to be fused
In the fission of rising sap
About to burst.

Hush!
The winter lambs
Have already heard the earth rumblings
Of the first buds
Of their first
And for many
Only Spring.

For Eileen

Dandelions have gone into a
Frenzy on the lush
Spring lawn
Where Daisies segregate
Themselves in lively abundance.

On the finely clipped and smart hedgerows,
Primroses garland the roadside edge
In a thick bank of pale yellow and green.

Cowslips and Buttercups
Budding branches
And baby lambs.

This is a certain Spring.
More distinct than the last few
Muddled years.
The winter was cold
As of old.
It needed some energy
To see through to Spring.

Eileen didn't make it
And I'll miss her.

Four Seasons

And would this Spring
Touch its source
And reap its hard earned freedom,
That the Summer be decanted
In honeycombs that glisten
With nurturing joy.

And this Autumn rust renew
The golden carpet mulched
In grief and grandeur,
That Winter will embed
The hibernating will
Of cocooned dreams
And staggering life.
-
The broad rim of my vision
Eyes the fallow ground
In unnerving anticipation,
Once a breeze glance
Of arrogant and bountiful youth.

An Archive world

Outside the window the constant
Flurry of the breeze
Intimates at the dreakiness of the day.

Sheets of drizzle gossamer-like float
Across the courtyard in waves.

This room is silent though except
For the ticking of a hidden clock.

There is a musty smell of damp,
Of old maps and archives
In this parish history room.

An old and new computer are
Hemmed in by big piles of folders and
Ledgers waiting to be sorted.

Pictures of old trees and orchards
Line the walls between stacks
Of Ordinance survey maps.

Wonderful names of apple fruit,
Cornish Pine and Terry Knight,
Pig's Nose and Sydney Strake.
Lady's Fingers, Venus Pippin,
Hocking's Green and Sops in Wine.

Delicious names, Veitch's Perfection
That gild the grey day and outer world
In full balance with a reverence
For the spirit of nature's
Golden sap.

These names are an archive world
Of a bygone age,
Of a cultivation and conservation
Beyond the standby world
Of Plug and Save.

There are no false economies
In the ledgers of these spirits,
No shock and awe to challenge
The majesty of a single leaf
Or a new day's breathe.

Here in this archive room
Where there is time for history
Where the shelves need dusting
Where nothing is deleted
By the click of a button
Where everything becomes
Cardboard dust to my senses.
Time is but a hidden clock.

Dignity in Death

Over the root and bough
Strewn, knotted head
Of the bank
We descended.

The sleet was falling
Heavily but graced
The water's head
A thousand, thousand
Gentle kisses
Beneath us.

We waded in.

The sheep was dead,
Its bulk a boulder
On the river bed.
Its head at rest
A milky, mottled mask of death.
Its wool was webbed in flakes.
Its underside a marsh bed miasma.

We barely hesitated
As we dragged it out
Of its watery grave
And up the bank
To rest against a moss-clad
Tree trunk.

And there we left it,
Warmed in perverse
City wisdom,
And heartfelt compassion
To a seemingly better
Cemetery.

Alex and Jessica
In their young minds
Would remember our
Deed and not the death,
With no thoughts of
The cold Scottish night
And the rotting carcass,
Warm as they would be
In their beds.

Oh! that nature at one calling
Should both be cherished and damned
With such dignity in death.

Discomfort and disquiet

She lays on her sun-lounge
Simmering in the sweltering
Heat—suburban mother
With her black bikini
And creosote tan.

Across the lush cool lawn
Still dank from another day's rain,
An impertinent blackbird
Zigzags near,
Pecking this way and that,
Seemingly feckless and full
Of airs.

It stops then takes flight.

A thrush steals its place,
Only to be disturbed
By a pair of grey squirrels
Fusing the nearby trees
With their lively spark.

A passing jet overwhelms
The chatter of birds.

The woman scans the sky
For the silver sprite
Before the heat and light of the
Midday sun
Turns her on its spit,
Face down against the sun-lounge.

In the long lapse of quiet
That ensues,
Her back burns
Her forehead sweats,
And unnoticed,
Her young son approaches
Nervously and somewhat
Embarrassed.

The shadows we cast

The man is tall and upright,
Carries a brief case up the steps
To the front door. His head is part
Bald, his jacket black. He has the
Air of a mission, all stiffened
Resolve. Quite what he will deliver
I'm not sure. I don't envy him his
Visit, his calling card. He looks
Too young to cast judgement, too brittle
To fashion hope from a lost cause.
His brief case is a funeral parlour this I know.

My neighbour used to walk
The little dog piecemeal
Around the streets,
His long slow shadow
The dog's small feet.
Neither with particular
Strength of lungs.
He would say hello
If you fell upon him
But otherwise he'd leave alone,
Patience only for the dog
To discharge its scent,
His distance and diffidence
I could respect.
We left each other's world alone.

Over the last month his wife
Has walked the dog
And now his daughters are here.
Two visiting nurses in uniform
Called yesterday.
All this quiet activity at the door,
No sound of a bell from where
I stand.
Someone is dying,
I can sense who but I can't see in.
I have no wish to trespass,
Such are the shadows we cast.

Stone-Age Boys

They were stone-age boys,
Engineers of adventure
And construction,
Raised up on a bomb-site
To play amongst the paraphernalia,
Where weeds and tall-grass
Had clothed the rubble
And the pit-falls for twisted ankles
And bloody knees.

But they carried their scars,
These boys
As they might carry medals,
Proud emblems of the risks
They ran:-
Always the unexpected and sometimes
The rival gang
That threatened their territory
From beyond the desolate trees
That lined the borders.

And up these trees
These boys would drag
The wood and the nails
To build their look-out posts
And hideouts,
And beneath corrugated roofs
In their tree-top cradles
They reigned supreme.

No girls were allowed
Near this world,
To hold things up
Or shed too many tears
When hit by an enemy stone
Or a lurking fear.

Only the wind could interfere:—

The wind that blew from the sea
And sent clouds
Racing across the deep blue sky,
But not even the cold air
Or the rain could make
These boys blue.

There was nothing to demolish then
You see,
No tin-can dreams
On rubbish tip scree.
Only a world to fill
And a life to strut
Among the stinging nettles
And the wooden huts.

Wooden huts?

Yes, those with picks and shovels in
That suddenly appeared
One morning with the dumper-trucks,
When an empire collapsed
Bulldozed into oblivion
Without warning, without fight.

And what scars
Could they then show?
These Stone-Age boys.
What could they know
About concrete
And redbrick
And washing-line rights?
They were raised to live and to fight,
With wooden shields
And all their might.

But there were scars,
Scars they dared not show,
And dreams to follow
Yet nowhere to go,
Nowhere, these days
Should the hard rain blow.

Whitsand Bay memories

In one thought
I'd been bowled down the beach steps
To the crunchy sands
Pitted in the heat of summer's
Midday trek.
There with a throng of thirsty souls
We came lapping
Dog like in search of the clear horizon.

What did we find there?
What do we ever find?

—Sand flies on the tar-sweating rocks,
A sun so hot it blisters any thought,
A sea so clumsy and drunk
It fills each gulping mouth
With salt.

And yet we happily fooled
About in the sea and sand,
There on the wide expanse.
Do you remember?
Whitsand Bay on a Sunday afternoon?

God, I thirsted after you then
And though you told me not
To be silly this only increased my
Panic and desire.

Only later could I understand
The distance in your words
Though my senses were true.

Yet even now I wonder
If you were so still
As you flowed past me;—

The sound of water over rock.

And I wonder in flickering
Moments,
In a youthful recess
What trickle of a memory
Flows through your blood.
And what kind of waters are washed at your
Feet all theses years on?

Tamar Night

Down a winding gravel track
Past the barbed wire fences
And clumps of fir trees is a creek
On the Cornwall side of the Tamar
Ria near Anthony Passage.

Here broken tree trunks
Sunken into the mud
Used to case a rusted jetty,
Where once I threw knives
With a gypsy boy
At a workman's wooden hut,
And gazed in awe at the Battleship
Vanguard at rest.

From this vantage point
You could watch the warships
Re-fuelling at the end
Of a long causeway jetty,
Studded but treacherously
Slippery with the wax
Of oil and seawater.

I walked this causeway
A few times to my father's
Ship and behind one,
Eerie and silent,
Stood massive oil dumps
Nestled on the hillside
Amongst the trees.

In those days further up the river
Beyond Brunel's bridge,
Were moored black ammunition barges,
Bobbing and bathing
In the afternoon sunlight.
Next to them stood mighty
Yellow and black tugs
Which once shoved Repulse
And Renown out beyond
The Sound.

Just below the bridge,
Anchored and moth-balled,
Were several old Battle class
Destroyers and not unusually
An aircraft carrier.
Now a posse of yachts and small craft clutter
The Saltash reach.

Along with the steam engines
That trundled across
Brunel's one-track masterpiece,
The soot and smoke of Great Britain's
Imperial scheme have faded
Into the Tamar night.

Suspension bridge and all
The Torpoint ferry
Still does good business
As it clunks and rattles
Across its sea-bed chain
To the Plymouth side.

This evening I got out
Of my car and stood
On the ferry top-deck
As of old and gazed
At what was left of the fleet
At rest, enchanted by the flicker of
Ships lights on the oily water.

Our departure was delayed
And suddenly with its escort of
Pilot boat and tugs a big black
Shape slid by us mid-river,
Like a giant cetacea of the night
And all the Tamar memories
Of awe and menace
Which held a young boy
In its grip came flooding
Back as I shivered
In the chill night breeze.

Soon I'd seen enough and descended
With mixed emotions
To the car ready to collect
My pound ticket and
To depart, without epiphany,
Into the Tamar night.

Virtue and Terror

Back in those Brylcreem days
Of Enid Blyton skies,
Eagle comics and Famous Five heroics,
I'd take myself off to the local barbers
Only a snip away from my
Mod credentials and James Dean
Smokey eyes.

I was a ten year old adult then
Without my mother's hand
And high board kiddies chair.
The barber's drape of a man's world
Hiding my sweaty palms
And tangled pretences.
My fluffy sideburns a give away,
As the silky hair of youth fell lightly
In those hallowed days of peace and progress.

One day, whilst in the waiting queue,
I took up a copy of Look and Learn
To see a picture of Maximilian Robespierre
All powder puffed and dandy like.
A sea-green incorruptable,author
Of the Terror so it said, close-bosom friend
Of the Peoples' Will and the Virtue of Madame Guillotine.

Would things were that clear-cut,
But there in that barber's chair
Such words and deeds were pages away.

Yet something scraped my innocent emotions
Like the barber's razor on my skin,
Though the only terror
I knew then was the transient fear
Of the scissors clipping
My ear,
Or the blushing embarrassment
Of too close a scrutiny
In the full-frontal mirror.

Reflections came later
With all the refractions
Of experience.

And sitting there in A-level lessons
With the words of Keats and Shelley
Ringing in my ears and the
Deeds of Marat and Danton
On my pen.
Citizen Robespierre and the Jacobins
Came again.

These were the pastel shades of a mid 60's
Trend, Impressionable Romantics, Larry J and I
Paraded around in our girlfriends' dandy frock coats,
Revolutionary turquoise blue and green,
Too tight to fit a Committee of
Public Safety insecure in an adolescent
Party scene, where the Small Faces
Gave way to Hendrix and Cream.

Yet no blood was shed with our
foolhardy mimicking. Romance
And Revolution were just games,
And Judgement before the Supreme Being
Was a multitude of cuts away.

Yet I edged closer,
There in a degree level exam hall,
Musing on the balmy days of July 1794
When Maximilian froze at the height of power,
When the Terror became his fear
And Virtue a knife's edge away from dictatorship.

What image betrayed him
Before the mirror of revolution
And Egalite?

The Fraternity of bloodshed
And the Liberty of conscience
Became his graves before
The days of Thermidor
And the grape shot of Napoleon's
Canons in democracy's wake.

"Je suis la revolution"

Yes! I am the Revolution.

This I came to understand.
Though I dribbled in the wind
And wept in corners,
Struggled for breath
In the fast race of life
When History became blood
On my hands,
The Terror a face of
A starving child
And Virtue a monk on fire
Burning to a cinder.

I am the Revolution
Though I only keep watch
As I guard the castle in these choleric days,
Where no quarter is
Given and multitudes
Trundle to their graves
Needlessly before their time.

In some strange way my watchfulness
Has become the virtue of my humanity
And the terror of my insignificance.
I, the Committee of Public
Safety, there in my hairdresser's
Chair where John my barber
Talks to me in the full-frontal mirror,
His Danton-like pox-pitted face
Staring in reflection at my
Quiet attentiveness.

Am I musing like Robespierre on my next
Move?

No!
I am not handcuffed to any peoples' will
Like him and I have accused myself
Many times for my mortal sins.

More like I freeze for what to say
As John reminisces on 'better days'
Where music was not hip-hop
And glam-assed in your face,
When he was a rocker
In the clear cut
Cold War days.

"Religion,
A shit on it all," he mutters.
"Terrorists, extremists,
Fucking bastards,
Nutters all."

He raises the razor to the light
And I would tremble
Were he St Just the
Avenging Angel of Death
And my head a retribution for
Lack of virtue and ineffectiveness.
But this is not my lot and
I have no terror,
No sweaty palm,
No blushing embarrassment
Now in the full-frontal mirror,
So many are the cuts.
Just the eyes of an executioner
And the heart of Christ.
The one a virtue the other
A guillotine vice.

Virtue and Iniquity

"But she hath lost a dearer thing than life." The Rape of Lucrece.—William Shakespeare

The night is dark,
This ungodly hour.
What virtue breeds, iniquity
Stalks in heinous guise
To devour.

—————

A young girl bleeds
In the stolen car
That takes her anywhere,
Anyway,
Into the drugged up night.

She dreams of her father
And of hapless children
Coughing violent phlegm
Into the lenses of cameras
That nurse the world
With sugar.

She sees the flashy ring
On his trigger-happy finger
As she drifts to the beaches
And the sea-spray wind
That blows fierce and free
Through the open window.

The screech of the seagull
Is the cry of her heart
Ascending from the wrench
Of flesh glued to
The polyester seat.

She feels the cold and heat
As she rustles her strength
To the factory of eyes
And the goatish grins
That ever expand
Towards her.

She knows no sound
But the violence of hysteria
Mingling with the grinding
Of bones and descent
Into nausea.

She rinses her spit with the cake of sweat
And hair,
Feels the bruise of an elbow
In her neck as she chokes
On his vinegar breath.

She reaches out
For the gentle hand
That will guide her
Through the passages
Of unconsciousness
As she senses her body
Severed from its head.

The cries now riveted in her eyes.
The scalding acid on her chafed
And wounded thighs.
Almond milk and honey,
The song of paradise.

Nothing will ever be the same
Again for her.
Nothing but the pain and the shame.

Avalon

"And near him stood the Lady of the Lake
Who knows a subtler magic than his own." Idylls of the King.—Alfred, Lord Tennyson

Winter muffles the lake.

A sudden gust of wind
Shoves the water
Bellowing into the marsh grass.

It doesn't last.

He faces her face then faces the pale sun,
Shrill and silent
Over the wide expanse
And barren are the hills
That lead from this pebble shore.

"Wear that withered hand in your coat
My love
By the tree where you stand.

Oh! The things forsaken in our looks
And how we know.

Come breathe,
Touch my skin once more
Though desolate eyes are watching us."

She turns aside to touch the island shore
Across the water
So deep he cares not to follow.

She sheds a look on the stony ground
As he turns around.

"It's cold." She mutters
and there's no escape.

A moment of prayer.

On Cape Greco, Cyprus,
near Anargroi Cave, a little white chapel
stands with its French blue shutters and doors
and two pin-point crosses at either end
of its semi-cylindrical roof.
The building sparkles in the Egyptian sun.

Inside it is dark and cool,
lit only with one bare light bulb.

In front of the frescoed altar frieze
I light a candlewick in an oil filled
jam-jar and kneel and pray as I did
as a little boy. Orthodox saints watch over me.

Now there is only one heart that hears me.
One heart that is in my presence.

Outside the wind blows the sea
against the craggy shoreline.
The bright morning sun
is beginning to warm the pink,
chalky earth.
By the cave the sea pits and flutes
the promontory rocks in excited dalliance.
Spits of foam anoint my brow.

A lone bird flits past
and perches on a picnic bench.
Red, white and blue fishing buoys
are anchored tight in the choppy shunt of waves.

On the Cape, distant radar pylons ladder the sky and beacon
a world beyond my eyes and the peppered dust
of my imagination squinting as it does into the sharp sun.

And as I turn to leave my moment of prayer,
there is only one hand that holds me now,
that holds me here as the candlewick light
in the chapel floats and flickers in its oily jam jar sea,
to be extinguished sooner or later.

Only ghosts roam free

"I saw him lying in a gutter
across a path of flowing blood,
I thought to stop and ask him
The nature of his love,
But as I kneeled the rain stopped
And in the cold night I stood and groped."

We rot in these
Pits
These mud-slime
Pits
And the incessant rain
Of Gaul,
Blow our noses
Free of cordite grime
Clasp our hands
In the shiver
Of moonlight
And look to God
In our likeness.

He lay there
Bemused,
Coiled in barbed wire
And surrounded
By ghosts
Breathing fire in the night.

At daylight
we saw him
moth-hooked
and dripping of dew.

We heard the dull
Thud of blood
Oozing from
Its festered vessel.

We simplified
His memory
In the long queue
Of heroes
And asked what name he carved
Amongst friend and foe,
What life he
Owned in the huts
He staked,
In the seeds
He sowed
In the sylvan
Wilds of Gaul.

And we kissed
The moss,
Hugged the mist
And the fern bank bliss
Of the wood thrushes
Song,
Saw what likeness
Was struck
To the clank of iron
And glint
Of bronze
In the strong ordeal
Of battle.

At daylight
We saw
Them dripping
With dew.

We heard the dull
Thud of jackboots
Passing through.

We asked how long
We must wait bemused
Surrounded
By ghosts
Breathing fire
In the night.

And they told us
We choked in those pits
Those concrete pits
And the incessant
Rain over Gaul,
Blew the snowflake
Dust from
Our noses,
Clasped our hands
In the skeleton moonlight
And looked to God
In our likeness.

The Doomsday Clock is a symbolic clock face that the 'The Bulletin of the Atomic Scientists' has maintained since 1947 at its headquarters on the campus of the University of Chicago. By 1984, at the height (or nadir) of the Reagan-Brezhnev era, the clock read three minutes to midnight. Cold war tensions had returned with an acceleration in the arms race, the Soviet invasion of Afghanistan, and the continued intransigence toward political and economic reform within the Soviet bloc, such as the imposition of martial law in Poland. Would Europe become a battleground yet again? This poem was written at that time. Recently the clock was changed from 7minutes to 5 minutes to midnight.

Appendix

Acknowledgements and notes

I have not dated the poems in this collection. Most are of fairly recent origin or reworking. However, a few date from either the 70's or the 80's.

Of a night like this

"tremulous and tender" comes from the song 'Music of the Night' by Andrew Lloyd Weber.

Catering for the bad taste cooks.

This is a very old poem of mine and is a collage of images gleaned mostly from a food article from the Times in, I think,1978. I cannot acknowledge the source as I should because I did not keep a record.

Adios 2and 3

'Tin Soldier' was released on December 1st 1967 and was the Small Faces' 11th single. It is regarded by many as the finest recording by this great '60's British group.

There are many references in literature to wild regret. In Adios 3 I'm indebted to Leonard Cohen for his use of wild regret in the song 'The Faith' and the phrase "solitude of strength" in the song 'The Letters.' Both tracks are on the 'Dear Heather' album by Leonard Cohen.

Virtue and Iniquity

In the opening stanza I have adapted Shakespeare who writes 'What virtue breeds iniquity devours.' The Rape of Lucrece.

Avalon

Avalon, the mythical island, Avalon, the ideal; the pursuit of beauty and passion, wonderment and high aspirations in a world too often malevolent and mediocre. Avalon, the island of hope? A daunting prospect.

The author gratefully acknowledges the inspiration offered to him by the fragments of these artists' and writers' work and to those quoted elsewhere in the book.